Reorienting U.S. Pakistan Strategy
From Af-Pak to Asia

COUNCIL *on* **FOREIGN RELATIONS**

Council Special Report No. 68
January 2014

Daniel S. Markey

Reorienting U.S. Pakistan Strategy
From Af-Pak to Asia

The Council on Foreign Relations (CFR) is an independent, nonpartisan membership organization, think tank, and publisher dedicated to being a resource for its members, government officials, business executives, journalists, educators and students, civic and religious leaders, and other interested citizens in order to help them better understand the world and the foreign policy choices facing the United States and other countries. Founded in 1921, CFR carries out its mission by maintaining a diverse membership, with special programs to promote interest and develop expertise in the next generation of foreign policy leaders; convening meetings at its headquarters in New York and in Washington, DC, and other cities where senior government officials, members of Congress, global leaders, and prominent thinkers come together with Council members to discuss and debate major international issues; supporting a Studies Program that fosters independent research, enabling CFR scholars to produce articles, reports, and books and hold roundtables that analyze foreign policy issues and make concrete policy recommendations; publishing *Foreign Affairs*, the preeminent journal on international affairs and U.S. foreign policy; sponsoring Independent Task Forces that produce reports with both findings and policy prescriptions on the most important foreign policy topics; and providing up-to-date information and analysis about world events and American foreign policy on its website, CFR.org.

The Council on Foreign Relations takes no institutional positions on policy issues and has no affiliation with the U.S. government. All views expressed in its publications and on its website are the sole responsibility of the author or authors.

Council Special Reports (CSRs) are concise policy briefs, produced to provide a rapid response to a developing crisis or contribute to the public's understanding of current policy dilemmas. CSRs are written by individual authors—who may be CFR fellows or acknowledged experts from outside the institution—in consultation with an advisory committee, and are intended to take sixty days from inception to publication. The committee serves as a sounding board and provides feedback on a draft report. It usually meets twice—once before a draft is written and once again when there is a draft for review; however, advisory committee members, unlike Task Force members, are not asked to sign off on the report or to otherwise endorse it. Once published, CSRs are posted on www.cfr.org.

For further information about CFR or this Special Report, please write to the Council on Foreign Relations, 58 East 68th Street, New York, NY 10065, or call the Communications office at 212.434.9888. Visit our website, CFR.org.

To submit a letter in response to a Council Special Report for publication on our website, CFR.org, you may send an email to CSReditor@cfr.org. Alternatively, letters may be mailed to us at: Publications Department, Council on Foreign Relations, 58 East 68th Street, New York, NY 10065. Letters should include the writer's name, postal address, and daytime phone number. Letters may be edited for length and clarity, and may be published online. Please do not send attachments. All letters become the property of the Council on Foreign Relations and will not be returned. We regret that, owing to the volume of correspondence, we cannot respond to every letter.

This report is printed on paper that is FSC® certified by Rainforest Alliance, which promotes environmentally responsible, socially beneficial, and economically viable management of the world's forest.

Contents

Foreword

For more than a decade, U.S. strategy toward Pakistan has been dominated by the struggle against terrorism. The war launched in 2001 in neighboring Afghanistan and waged, in part, in Pakistan's tribal regions has overshadowed America's other interests in South Asia, not least nuclear issues, regional stability, and economic growth. Today, as the United States "rebalances" its foreign policy focus toward Asia, and as the U.S. military draws down its presence in Afghanistan, the relationship between the United States and Pakistan is poised for reassessment. The outcome, however, is anything but clear. A clean break between Pakistan and the United States seems unlikely, despite simmering disagreements over a number of issues. Also unlikely is a full rapprochement. That said, if it chose to do so, Pakistan could contribute to the advancement of U.S. priorities in Asia, Afghanistan, and the war on terror, but the country's weak governance, slow economic growth, and growing nuclear arsenal combine to cast serious doubt on whether it will so choose.

In this Council Special Report, Daniel S. Markey examines Pakistan's complex role in U.S. foreign policy. Markey advocates a two-pronged U.S. approach to Pakistan that works to confront and quarantine the immediate threats it poses to regional security and stability while simultaneously attempting to integrate it into the broader U.S. agenda in Asia.

Regional security is with good reason the first prong of Markey's strategy. The destructive potential of a weakened, isolated, and/or hostile Pakistan is, he writes, significant. An armed conflict between India and Pakistan, or a major Pakistan-based terror attack on India, would not only disrupt India's booming economy but also affect wider regional stability. Pakistan's internal security threats, Markey notes, are no less serious, and the possibility that it will continue to offer safe haven to terrorist organizations, imperil Afghanistan's reconstruction, or disrupt U.S. negotiations with the Taliban is a source of real concern.

Markey recommends that the United States act now to address these threats and work to contain the effects of Pakistan's domestic challenges within its borders. He suggests that the United States open a formal dialogue with China's Ministry of Foreign Affairs on Pakistan issues and explore options for expanded counterterror cooperation with India. Markey also proposes that the United States restructure its military aid to Pakistan, decoupling it from the war in Afghanistan and focusing (as well as conditioning) it instead on Pakistan's efforts to fight terrorism and violent extremism within its borders.

In pursuit of regional integration, the second prong of his strategy, Markey recommends that the United States create opportunities for Pakistan to develop relationships with its neighbors in Asia, particularly India. He calls for a trade agreement with India, Afghanistan, and Pakistan that would offer preferential access to American markets on the condition that those countries reduce barriers to intraregional trade. He also recommends that the United States support the Turkmenistan-Afghanistan-Pakistan-India pipeline project and, more broadly, that Washington focus its civilian aid on other trade-related infrastructure such as roads, bridges, and ports. The economic and strategic benefits of integration could be substantial. Markey explores several scenarios in which, for example, more normal relations with India could enable Pakistan to act as a regional trade hub or even contribute to regional security.

In the pages that follow, Markey offers useful recommendations for a revamped U.S.-Pakistan strategy. The result is a valuable report that, while emphasizing the urgent need to combat the many threats Pakistan poses, nonetheless provides a glimpse of what a more integrated Pakistan could in turn contribute to Asia. It is a vision well worth considering, if only because the alternatives could prove so costly.

Richard N. Haass
President
Council on Foreign Relations
January 2014

Acknowledgments

I would like to thank CFR President Richard N. Haass and Director of Studies James M. Lindsay for their support of this project, and especially for their perceptive feedback throughout the editorial process.

I am grateful to the members of my advisory committee, starting with its chair, James Shinn, who graciously and effectively presided over our meetings in Washington, DC. Astute insights from the group forced me to consider—and often to reconsider—the assumptions behind my arguments and to explore their implications for U.S. policy in ways I might otherwise have missed.

I owe a debt of gratitude to the many U.S., Indian, Chinese, and Pakistani policymakers who, over the past several years, have entertained discussions about the future of the U.S.-Pakistani relationship in a broader regional context. Special thanks go to Pakistan's embassy in Washington, DC, for helping to arrange interviews in Pakistan, including an informative session at Pakistan's National Defense University.

As always, working with my colleagues at CFR has been a pleasure. Patricia Dorff and Eli Dvorkin in Publications provided smart, careful, and quick edits of every draft. They could not have been more helpful. Behind the scenes, the Studies, Communications, and CFR.org teams made everything else possible from conception to rollout.

This report owes a great deal to the hard work, enthusiasm, and keen intellect of my research associate, Kevin Grossinger. Along the way, several impressive CFR interns have also assisted with research, including Sikander Kiani, Mashal Shah, Harris Rothman, and James West.

This publication was made possible by a grant from the John D. and Catherine T. MacArthur Foundation. The statements made and views expressed are solely my own.

Daniel S. Markey

Council Special Report

Introduction

After 9/11, the global fight against al-Qaeda and the related war in Afghanistan forced the United States to reassess its strategy in Pakistan. The exigencies of counterterrorism and counterinsurgency established Washington's primary goals and many of its specific policies. Now, however, the impending drawdown of U.S. troops from Afghanistan, along with significant U.S. successes in operations against al-Qaeda, require the United States to take a fresh look at its Pakistan strategy and to move beyond the "Af-Pak" era.

Washington is playing for high stakes in Pakistan. Pakistan's rapidly growing population of nearly two hundred million, expanding nuclear arsenal, political turmoil, entrenched terrorist networks, and internal violence mean that it will continue to draw the attention of U.S. policymakers well into the future. There can be no exit from or quick fix for the welter of thorny challenges Pakistan presents. Therefore, the goal of the United States should be to defend against immediate threats while keeping the door open to cooperative ventures that hold the promise of delivering to Pakistan greater security, economic growth, and normalized relations with its neighbors over the long term.

In addition to Pakistan-specific concerns, policymakers in Washington will need to determine how best to factor Pakistan into the broader U.S. agenda in Asia. That agenda is a long and multifaceted one, but it ultimately hinges on perpetuating and expanding the region's economic success. Continued growth, in turn, requires a long-term U.S. capacity to respond effectively to the reality of growing Chinese power, most obviously in the economic sphere but also increasingly in the military and diplomatic arenas. The bilateral relationship between the United States and China is the driving force behind the Obama administration's "rebalancing" strategy; it has prompted a renewed U.S. commitment to regional treaty allies like Japan and it has energized ties between the United States and newer Asian partners, including India.

In Washington, Pakistan has long been considered peripheral to "Asia," by which U.S. policymakers tend to mean East Asia and the Pacific. Yet the steady westward expansion of Chinese influence—starting with trade, transit, and investment—is likely to render that mental map all but outdated. Moreover, India's growing population, economy, and global diplomatic stature have already captured the imagination of U.S. strategic planners who no longer see India as a mere South Asian player, but as a major U.S. partner in Asia writ large. Severed from British India at its independence in 1947, Pakistan has a history of tension and hostility with modern-day India and of close friendship with neighboring China. These ties of history and geography make it impossible to disentangle Pakistan from the broader Asian landscape.

Yet, aside from the Obama administration's 2009 attempt to take a regional approach to Afghanistan (and, by extension, Pakistan), U.S. policymakers have not publicly clarified how they envision Pakistan's role in a wider regional context.[1] Nor have they explained how U.S. policies elsewhere in Asia should affect Pakistan itself or Washington's relationship with Islamabad.

In Islamabad, the U.S. rebalancing strategy is already widely interpreted as part and parcel of an impending U.S. abandonment of Pakistan, tilt toward India, and effort to contain China—all unwelcome developments from Islamabad's point of view. These concerns are likely to exacerbate Islamabad's sense of insecurity and widen existing rifts with Washington. That, in turn, would harm U.S. efforts to address immediate security concerns (starting with the threats posed by Pakistan-based terrorist groups) and to build cooperation in ways that would lead Pakistan to play a more constructive role in the region over time.

Pakistan's internal trajectory—whether toward a positive future of greater security and economic growth, a continued muddle of slow growth and dysfunctional politics, or a negative spiral of violence—will also affect its neighbors, including India and China. At risk are the U.S. interests in crafting an expanded partnership with an India that is strong, prosperous, and capable of contributing to regional and global security; avoiding a possible new flash point for conflict with China; and escaping major crises and similar distractions that would suck Washington's attention and resources from initiatives to promote U.S. commercial and diplomatic projects in the rest of Asia.

To implement a new Pakistan strategy that focuses greater U.S. attention on links with wider Asia, Washington should take a two-pronged approach that effectively quarantines Pakistan-based threats to Asian security even as it creates new opportunities to integrate Pakistan into the region's vibrant economy. To do so, Washington would need to reorganize its policymaking structure to reintegrate Pakistan into wider Asia. Among other policy initiatives, the strategy would include launching a new U.S. diplomatic dialogue with Beijing, New Delhi, and Islamabad to reduce prospects for regional tension and violence; signing a U.S. trade deal to encourage trade between India and Pakistan; and reallocating U.S. assistance programming in Pakistan to improve trade and transit infrastructure.

U.S. Interests in Asia

The primary U.S. interest in Asia is to maintain and advance prospects for a peaceful, secure order conducive to U.S. and global economic growth. Asian economies are engines of global expansion, opportunities for U.S. investment, and pillars of the international monetary and financial system. China, Japan, and South Korea are, for instance, the second-, fourth-, and seventh-largest U.S. trading partners.[2] China and Japan hold well over $2 trillion in U.S. Treasury securities.[3]

The Obama administration signaled its appreciation of the U.S. interest in Asia by announcing plans in late 2011 for a strategy of "rebalancing." The new approach was expressed in President Barack Obama's remarks to the Australian parliament in November 2011 and Secretary of State Hillary Clinton's article, "America's Pacific Century," published in *Foreign Policy* the same month.[4] As Clinton wrote, "strategically, maintaining peace and security across the Asia-Pacific is increasingly crucial to global progress."

At the heart of any U.S. strategy for promoting peace, security, and economic growth in Asia is the relationship with China. As Beijing translates decades of stunning economic growth into international influence and military might, the United States has attempted to balance between two goals. On the one hand, Washington seeks mutually beneficial cooperation, especially with respect to trade and investment where the two economies are deeply interdependent. On the other hand, Washington also competes with Beijing for regional and global influence, supports allies that feel threatened by Chinese power, and hedges against the possibility that Beijing will use its growing power to undermine specific U.S. initiatives or, more generally, the principles and institutions that form the core of the U.S.-led, postwar international order. An effective U.S. strategy would, at minimum, encourage Beijing to cooperate whenever possible, play by mutually agreeable rules in competitive circumstances, and address other differences peacefully.

Effective diplomacy with China, then, is a necessary precondition for Asian peace and economic growth. Such diplomacy typically takes place in bilateral settings like the recent "shirtsleeves summit" of June 2013, but U.S.-China relations do not exist in a vacuum. By working with powerful states throughout the region, the United States will have a better chance to counterbalance Chinese power, if not necessarily to restrict or contain it. The United States thus has an enduring interest in strengthening alliances with states like Japan and Korea and cultivating partnerships with states like Vietnam and Singapore, both on their own merits and in part as a means to improve U.S. leverage with Beijing.

Hence the Obama administration's desire, expressed in the rebalancing strategy, to project a more visible and active presence in Asia. That presence includes heightened negotiations on the Trans-Pacific Partnership (TPP) free trade agreement, U.S. participation in the Association of Southeast Asian Nations (ASEAN)–affiliated East Asia Summit, a new contingent of U.S. Marines stationed in Australia, and an increased naval presence in Singapore, among other initiatives.[5]

Along similar lines, the United States has sought to cultivate closer ties with India in recognition of its significance in the region and its vast potential as a U.S. partner in Asia.[6] Washington is not merely interested in forging a better relationship with New Delhi; top U.S. officials in the Obama administration have been unequivocal in their desire to contribute to India's economic and military expansion.[7] To be sure, the United States would have an interest in good relations with an enormous Asian country like India regardless of whether it was also seeking to influence China. Yet there can be little doubt that shared apprehensions about how Beijing will use its newfound wealth and power have brought Washington and New Delhi closer together.

Given the U.S. interest in Asia's economy, Washington would be concerned about the potential for regional security crises whether or not they were directly connected with China. That said, flash points with the potential to exacerbate U.S.-China frictions—like the Taiwan Strait, North Korea, and maritime disputes in the South China Sea—assume added geopolitical significance. The United States has a particular interest in preventing such crises or, if that proves impossible, in mitigating prospects for escalation that would place Washington in direct conflict with Beijing and jeopardize the global economy.

Pakistan's Role in Asia

Pakistan is implicated, if indirectly, in many of Washington's broader Asian concerns. The United States has an interest in Pakistan's security, prosperity, and regional relations because Pakistan has the potential to affect the region's economic growth, diplomacy between Washington and Beijing, and prospects for U.S.-India partnership. Given Pakistan's huge population (likely to top three hundred million by midcentury), geographic location, nuclear arms, and historical relationships with India and China, it is clear that a hostile or violently unstable Pakistan would compromise the broader U.S. agenda in Asia, whereas a cooperative, growing Pakistan would advance it.

It is difficult to predict Pakistan's future, as the range of plausible outcomes is vast and will be determined, first and foremost, by domestic developments largely beyond Washington's control. These potential futures range from anti-Western hostility and revolution to peaceful economic growth and democratic consolidation. In between is the muddled alternation of ineffective military dictatorship and civilian mismanagement, a condition in which Pakistan has languished for most of its history.[8]

Unfortunately, the current combination of massive population growth, abysmal education, and the gradual weakening of traditional institutions (both state and nonstate) makes it easier to imagine that Pakistan will be a net exporter of violence to its region rather than a net contributor to security. That said, Pakistan is not doomed to a downward slide; improvements in leadership and governance would enable the country to play a more constructive role over time.

PAKISTAN AS A THREAT
TO THE U.S. AGENDA IN ASIA

A hostile or destabilized Pakistan would upset U.S. plans in Asia simply by diverting Washington's attention and depleting U.S. resources. A serious security crisis in nuclear-armed Pakistan would capture Washington's attention and suck the air out of other U.S. policy initiatives until resolved. Pakistan's expanding nuclear program of more than one hundred warheads does not pose an existential threat to the United States of the sort posed during the Cold War by the Soviet Union's massive intercontinentally capable nuclear arsenal. However, if pieces of Pakistan's nuclear program were to fall into hostile hands, whether because future leaders in Islamabad take a more belligerent anti-U.S. stance or because Pakistan's nuclear materials and technologies leak to terrorist groups, then Washington would undoubtedly use military force and any other means necessary to deter and defend against their use on U.S. or allied targets.

Similarly, Pakistan-based terrorists and insurgents—including the remnants of al-Qaeda's core leadership, their sympathizers and affiliates, and regional terrorist organizations like the Afghan Haqqani network and Lashkar-e-Taiba (LeT)—threaten regional security and, by extension, Asian economic growth. Not all of these terrorist groups have yet demonstrated a capacity to strike the U.S. homeland, but they are clearly dedicated to attacking U.S. friends and allies in the region when the opportunity arises.

Motivated by the urgent need to degrade the capacity and global reach of al-Qaeda and its affiliates, the United States launched the war in Afghanistan, the drone campaign over Pakistani tribal areas, and a range of other regional counterterror activities, including covert intelligence operations and investigations of financial transactions. U.S. forces have successfully delivered a blow to al-Qaeda's top leadership in Pakistan and Afghanistan, but many of Pakistan's other militant and extremist organizations have grown more violent and sophisticated since 9/11. Some, like the Pakistani Taliban (TTP), now attack Pakistan's state institutions and civilians in ways that were inconceivable in prior decades and that raise doubts about Islamabad's capacity to maintain basic law and order, let alone to attract trade and investment in ways that would grow the national economy. Others, like LeT, persist in an old game of directing their violence beyond Pakistan's borders.

Pakistan's nuclear weapons and terrorist groups thus cast a cloud over the region's general security and economic outlook. Moreover, if Pakistan lurches toward greater regional hostility or violence, the shift could create trouble between Washington and Beijing or to undermine India's position as a major counterbalancing force in Asia, both of which would run counter to U.S. interests.

PAKISTAN AS AN IRRITANT IN U.S.-CHINA RELATIONS

A hostile Pakistan would contribute to friction between Washington and Beijing in ways that harm prospects for productive U.S.-China cooperation in other areas. Nuclear proliferation is an issue of particular concern. Chinese missile and nuclear designs have already played an important part in Pakistan's growing arsenal. Washington's desire to limit further proliferation of increasingly sophisticated Chinese technologies (by way of a hostile Pakistan) would lead U.S. officials into difficult exchanges with their Chinese counterparts of the sort that took place during the 1990s.[9] As a recent example, the Chinese have announced plans to finance two new nuclear reactors in Pakistan. The move has rankled U.S. policymakers who consider it a violation of China's obligations to the Nuclear Suppliers Group.[10]

New tensions of this sort will be more likely if Beijing and Islamabad pursue a relationship analogous to the one China has cultivated with North Korea. In that case, China would quietly encourage and abet Pakistan as a hostile force, perceiving Pakistan's utility as a dual buffer against the United States and India. In addition, China would use Pakistan as a vehicle for expanding its influence in Central Asia, Afghanistan, and other parts of the Muslim world. Chinese inroads into Pakistan, such as the Gwadar port along the Arabian Sea and the Karakoram Highway that links Pakistan to western China, would then assume greater strategic significance, permitting China to escape a U.S. naval chokehold along its eastern seaboard or to open a western naval front against India.

The risks to China of such an approach are plain, and this path is not consistent with recent policies from Beijing, which have tended to support Indo-Pakistani normalization and the avoidance, or, if necessary, the mitigation of crises in South Asia. Yet the possibility cannot be ruled out in the medium term, if only due to China's well-established history of supporting Pakistan to distract and unsettle India, and Pakistan's own long-standing desire to use China as an external balance against India.[11] Moreover, China would find it relatively easy to mask its strategic use of Pakistan in this way, claiming no responsibility for Islamabad's belligerence even if it encouraged such moves behind closed doors.

Just as the United States has an interest in making sure that spats with China's North Korean ward do not turn into direct conflicts with Beijing, Washington also has a stake in preventing the escalation of crises manufactured in Pakistan. It is hard to imagine that China or the United States would deliberately choose to escalate a U.S.-Pakistan crisis inspired, for instance, by a terrorist attack in the United States perpetrated by a group based in Pakistan. Even so, accidents and miscommunications would have the potential to push such contingencies in dangerous, unintended directions.

PAKISTAN AS A THREAT TO INDIA'S GROWTH

Even a marginal decrease in India's growth rate will prolong its developmental path and diminish its capacity to play a greater role in the world in ways Washington hopes to see in the decades to come, including with respect to balancing Chinese influence in Asia.

Recent history suggests that the primary means by which a hostile Pakistan would undermine India is through terrorism. An intense campaign of terrorist attacks in India by Pakistan-based groups would distract New Delhi and undermine national growth by scaring off investors and disrupting normal business operations. Such attacks have hurt India's economy in the past. In countries that routinely suffer from terrorism, like Israel, the costs to gross domestic product (GDP) can be significant.[12] Indo-Pakistani hostility has always imposed an economic drag on both countries, spurring them to divert scarce resources to arms buildups (including nuclear weapons) and away from other investments, such as infrastructure and education. Indo-Pakistani military mobilizations, such as those that occurred in 2001 and 2002, have imposed significant human and financial costs.[13]

India's long-term economic growth is already hampered by Pakistan's obstruction of overland access to energy resources in Central Asia. The persistence of political barriers to commerce with Pakistan, which would otherwise be as natural a trade and investment partner as Canada is to the United States, will retard India's growth.

The backdrop of persistent territorial disputes and deep distrust makes new Indo-Pakistani conflicts stemming from cross-border violence, proxy conflicts in Afghanistan, or access to water (particularly freshwater from the annual Himalayan glacier melt) quite plausible. And unlike early Indo-Pakistani wars (1947, 1965, 1971), any future conflict would have the potential to escalate past the nuclear threshold.[14] Resources that India allocates to addressing such military contingencies are not available for promoting economic development (infrastructure, education). Far worse, another major war with Pakistan would likely have devastating consequences on India's economy, undercutting U.S. interests by weakening India's role as an enhanced regional counterbalance to China's economic might.

PAKISTAN AS A CONSTRUCTIVE REGIONAL CONTRIBUTOR

Although there are many reasons to fear that Pakistan's daunting domestic challenges will lead it down a destructive path, there are also countervailing reasons to hope for an improved Pakistan that begins to confront challenges to security and development at home and is increasingly prepared to contribute to regional economic growth and peace.

For Pakistan to play such a constructive regional role, its civilian and military leaders would first need to implement economic reforms and build better administrative institutions. Islamabad would also need to take difficult steps to get its own house in order, starting by tackling its homegrown networks of violent extremism. A stable, strong Pakistan would deal a blow to dangerous terrorist groups and their affiliates operating in regions from Southeast Asia and western China to Central Asia and the Middle East.

If, for instance, Pakistan's leaders, including senior military officers, live up to their recent rhetoric about implementing a new national security strategy that prioritizes the need to tackle internal security threats, then they would be taking solid steps in this direction.[15] In this context, past U.S. military assistance has shown it can pay dividends; Pakistani military operations in the tribal areas along its border with Afghanistan have benefited from U.S. equipment and training. Although deep disagreements persist between Washington and Islamabad, the two sides have also achieved important military and counterterror successes on issues where they see eye to eye.

If Pakistan and India were to build sufficient trust to overcome past animosity and sufficient capacity to put down the armed groups that benefit from disrupting their trade and transit, Pakistan would offer a thoroughfare for Central Asian energy supplies—by way of pipelines or power lines—to feed the huge and increasing demand throughout South and Southeast Asia. Years of negotiations on energy pipelines through Pakistan to India (from Turkmenistan and Iran) provide ample evidence of India's eagerness to seize such opportunities despite its history of conflict with Pakistan.

Under such conditions, Pakistan would serve as an overland transit hub, linking new transit corridors that run both east-west and north-south. India is eager to build ties with the fast-growing states of ASEAN, and plans are already being hatched to construct networks of roads, rail lines, and air- and seaports linking the region all the way from Vietnam to Central Asia, and from there on to Europe.[16] At the same time, Beijing is working on a north-south route that connects western China through Pakistan to the Arabian Sea. These overlapping networks would create positive, mutually reinforcing incentives in Pakistan to upgrade infrastructure, improve its internal security and legal protections in ways that would offer greater confidence to foreign investors, and maintain peaceful relations with its neighbors.

Warmer relations with India would likewise free Pakistan's military to make broader regional security contributions, for instance, by expanding its participation in UN peacekeeping operations and the counterpiracy and counterterror task forces of the Combined Maritime Forces coalition based in Manama, Bahrain. Moreover, Pakistan's leaders would enhance their regional clout by lending military muscle to new and emerging multilateral Asian security initiatives, whether under the inclusive umbrella of the ASEAN Regional Forum or through other smaller, task-oriented groups. With all of these contributions, Pakistan would serve the broader U.S. goal of expanding Asian prosperity and contributing, if indirectly, to global and U.S. economic growth.

Finally, a cooperative, stable Pakistan would also advance the U.S. interest in responding effectively to China's regional influence and growing economic power. If the U.S.-China relationship continues to be marked by both geopolitical competition and cooperation, as is generally expected, Pakistan is unusually well positioned to play a non-aligned role, in which it would maintain ties with both Washington and Beijing and reap the benefits of each relationship without having to pick sides. In that case, Washington would be able to use contacts and access inside Pakistan to more easily track and respond to Chinese diplomatic, military, and commercial activities in South and Central Asia. If U.S.-China relations swing toward greater competition and conflict, the utility of that vantage point on China's western flank would grow. Alternatively, if U.S.-China relations trend toward warmer cooperation, Pakistan would be a good place for Washington and Beijing to practice working together in the service of regional economic growth and security.

Pakistan Strategy: Af-Pak Versus Asia

At issue is whether the United States is better off dealing with Pakistan through a bureaucratic and strategic framework that continues to prioritize connections with Afghanistan, or if it makes more sense for the United States to reorient its Pakistan strategy toward a wider Asian approach.

OPTION 1: CONTINUE AF-PAK STRATEGY

At present, U.S. strategy toward Pakistan remains primarily rooted in post-9/11 Af-Pak issues: the counterterror campaign and the war in Afghanistan. This strategic emphasis is also reflected in bureaucratic structures of policymaking in Washington, where the U.S. departments of State and Defense, as well as the National Security Staff, have all been reconfigured at various points during the past decade to improve coordination and expand resources for U.S. policies that span the Afghanistan-Pakistan border. To the extent that U.S. policy has considered Pakistan in a regional context, it has centered on Afghanistan, such as through the Regional Economic Cooperation Conferences or the "new silk road" scheme to increase trade and transit via Afghanistan into Central Asia.

The chief reason to continue pursuing this approach toward Pakistan is that the United States has considerable unfinished business in the Af-Pak portfolio. True, Washington has scored significant victories against al-Qaeda in Pakistan and Afghanistan. And come what may, the Obama administration has clearly resolved to downsize the U.S. military presence in Afghanistan over the course of 2014. Even so, the United States still has a long list of unmet goals for Pakistan that are directly related to the Af-Pak agenda of counterterrorism and war.

Washington's to-do list with Pakistan starts with the logistical puzzle of how to clear a vast inventory of U.S. supplies, vehicles, and equipment from Afghan battlefields. Pakistan's roads and ports offer the fastest, cheapest route home, but recent experience has taught the United States that it cannot take the unimpeded flow of war materiel through Pakistan for granted.[17] More generally, Islamabad will play an important role in determining whether even Washington's scaled-back ambitions for post-2014 Afghanistan will succeed. How Pakistan uses its relationships with Afghan Taliban leaders will, for instance, have a direct effect on the outcome of reconciliation talks pursued by both Kabul and Washington.

Even more contentious bilateral issues that have yet to be resolved include the persistence of international terrorist safe havens on Pakistani soil and the U.S. use of drones to attack them. In addition to al-Qaeda and its affiliates, Washington has grave concerns about other violent extremist organizations based in Pakistan, some of which—like Lashkar-e-Taiba—have enjoyed the support of the Pakistani military and intelligence services.

The Obama administration has backed its Af-Pak strategy with considerable resources. At the height of the U.S. military campaign in late 2010 and 2011, one hundred thousand U.S. troops surged into Afghanistan. Roughly half as many forces are now based in Afghanistan, but leaked documents suggest that Washington continues to devote enormous intelligence resources to the region's security threats.[18] Pakistan also remains one of the world's largest recipients of U.S. assistance, with FY2013 estimates of over $350 million in military and $800 million in civilian aid. Reimbursements for Pakistani military operations in support of the war in Afghanistan run close to $100 million per month. U.S. military assistance is principally intended to support Pakistan's capacity to fight internal security threats, whereas civilian aid is directed toward demonstrating the value of U.S.-Pakistan cooperation and enhancing Pakistan's security by helping Islamabad address its domestic challenges of energy, economic growth, stabilization, education, and health.[19]

OPTION 2: SHIFT TO A BROADER ASIAN STRATEGY

An Asia-centered strategy for Pakistan would have two substantive prongs, supported by a reconfigured policymaking bureaucracy that emphasizes Pakistan's ties to wider Asia rather than to Afghanistan. The first prong would include policies intended to ward off or quarantine Pakistan-based security threats. In contrast to the status quo, the primary emphasis would shift away from Afghanistan and toward the rest of Asia, where the United States will have considerably greater economic and strategic interests of its own over the long run. The second prong would be devoted to enhancing Pakistan's own security and development. Unlike the status quo, that effort would be advanced principally by working to integrate Pakistan into the positive economic developments of the Asian region, starting with trade and investment, rather than by way of large, direct U.S. assistance schemes.

Of course, the United States is already doing a great deal to address the security challenges that Pakistan's nuclear weapons, terrorists, and militant organizations pose to the wider region. Where Washington and Islamabad have found common cause—such as in fighting against Pakistan's homegrown Taliban insurgents—there would be no reason to alter the U.S. approach. In other cases, however, where U.S. intelligence gathering and covert operations are directed against threats the Pakistani state has been unwilling to tackle, such as the Haqqani network or LeT, Washington would need to reconsider the wisdom of remaining heavily dependent on U.S. personnel and facilities now based in Afghanistan. Over the long run (and perhaps much sooner if Washington is unable to negotiate a satisfactory bilateral security agreement with Kabul), maintaining a foothold in landlocked Afghanistan as a means to deal with Pakistan-based security threats is likely to be extraordinarily difficult and costly.

In light of Pakistan's geographic location, India is the obvious U.S. alternative to Afghanistan. In recent years, Washington and New Delhi have taken steps to expand their counterterror cooperation with the intention of building defenses against future attacks like the Lashkar-e-Taiba strike on Mumbai in November 2008.[20] However, given persistent terrorist threats and Pakistan's clear lack of capacity (and, in some cases, will) to tackle them, Washington would need to ramp up its efforts in India considerably, perhaps even to the point of establishing military and intelligence facilities on Indian soil. Yet any such plan would immediately run up against India's lingering ambivalence about tighter ties with the United States. A declared U.S. military/intelligence presence in India, even if directed against Pakistan-based security threats, is for now a political nonstarter in New Delhi, where Indian leaders jealously guard their freedom from binding alliances.[21]

Alternative U.S. basing arrangements on the Arabian Peninsula would likely prove more diplomatically feasible in the short-to-medium term. Even so, seeking closer cooperation with India on addressing Pakistan-based security threats would still be a high priority for Washington in the context of an Asia-centric Pakistan strategy. In addition to offering the best geographical vantage point for U.S. military and intelligence operations against Pakistan-based security threats, it would build closer working relationships that serve the broader U.S. goal of partnership with India.

To be clear, an Asia-oriented strategy toward Pakistan would suffer if it is defined primarily by an overt U.S. tilt toward India at Pakistan's expense. U.S. efforts to promote greater counterterror cooperation with India would therefore need to be complemented by diplomatic outreach to China. The main U.S. goal would be to encourage Beijing to counsel restraint in Islamabad. Fortunately, China's growing interest in a secure western frontier, concerns about violent extremism, and desire to expand commercial activities in India and Central Asia lead Beijing to share with Washington at least a basic desire to see Pakistan rein in its terrorists and reduce tensions with India.

More generally, any U.S. strategy focused narrowly on security threats will alienate Pakistanis and reinforce a dangerous hostility from Pakistan's elected and uniformed leadership. The second prong of the U.S. approach would therefore be defined by U.S. efforts to encourage Pakistan's integration into Asian markets and political-economic institutions as a means of growing Pakistan's economy and, by extension, improving its prospects for peace and regional cooperation. The Asian Development Bank (ADB) anticipates that 2013 will see 6.6 percent growth in the developing countries of Asia, well above Pakistan's 3.7 percent in 2012. If Pakistan can attract greater regional trade and investment, it would have a far better chance of benefiting from relatively low labor costs and gainfully employing its swelling young population rather than suffering from the social and political upheavals otherwise associated with a massive youth bulge. Not only would this improve prospects for Pakistan's internal security, it would also reduce the likelihood of Pakistan's becoming a spoiler of regional peace.

For Washington, the question is how best to help Pakistan integrate itself into the wider regional economy. The United States would need to approach the problem in two ways: first by creating incentives for Pakistan and its neighbors to break down existing political and regulatory barriers to trade and investment, and second by reallocating significant U.S. assistance and financing to infrastructure projects, such as roads, ports, and pipelines, that reduce the costs of trade and transit.

On the incentive side, Washington could, for instance, dangle the carrot of U.S. market access as a means to encourage Indo-Pakistani trade normalization. Some of the other U.S. development projects already under way in Pakistan, including hydroelectric dam projects, would continue to make sense as part of a general strategy to encourage regional investment in Pakistan's industrial sector. Energy shortages alone are estimated to have cost Pakistan as much as 4 percent of its GDP in recent years.[22]

WEIGHING THE OPTIONS

Shifting U.S. strategy on Pakistan would require diplomatic and pro-grammatic changes supported by a reorganized bureaucracy. The changes would undoubtedly create temporary disruptions and costs, but there are good reasons to believe the United States would still be better off adopting an Asia-oriented strategy for Pakistan and moving away from the present Af-Pak approach.

The principal problem with the Af-Pak strategy is that the United States' long-term commitment to Afghanistan's security is no longer credible from the Pakistani point of view. The Obama administra-tion's timetable for military drawdown and transfer of authority to Afghan forces in 2014 has sent the unmistakable signal to Islamabad that U.S. interests in Afghanistan are finite and dwindling. Other U.S. policy choices, such as leaving open the "zero option" for U.S. forces in Afghanistan after 2014, have further reinforced Pakistani expectations that a complete U.S. withdrawal is likely in the near future. Although U.S. diplomats and officers in Kabul routinely reject Pakistan's skepti-cal assessment of the U.S. commitment, the Pakistani view is consistent with the politics of the war back in the United States, where popular support has dried up and senior administration officials appear willing to accept the public's verdict.

In this context, a U.S. strategy that links Afghanistan and Pakistan also indicates the lack of a long-term U.S. interest in Pakistan. If 9/11 and the Afghan war brought the United States back to Pakistan after a decade of relative disinterest, the end of that war is, by Pakistani calculations, likely to lead to another period of U.S. abandonment. The on-again, off-again history of the U.S.-Pakistan relationship supports this conclusion, even as U.S. officials dutifully mouth their intentions to maintain an intense focus on Pakistan, both with respect to dealing with security threats and to fostering peace and economic growth.

The Obama administration's substantive and bureaucratic exclusion of Pakistan from its broader strategy for Asia compounds the U.S. commitment problem. Unlike neighboring India, for instance, Pakistan is conspicuously absent from official U.S. pronouncements about the rebalancing. And Washington's policies are consistent with its rhetoric. For instance, nascent U.S. initiatives to promote regional integration across South and Southeast Asia, such as the Indo-Pacific Economic Corridor, end at the Indian border. A similar point holds for other U.S. security initiatives in Asia, which are increasingly likely to include India, but never Pakistan.[23]

As a consequence, policymakers and analysts in Islamabad have been left to draw their own conclusions about U.S. intentions in Asia and how those intentions will guide U.S. policies in Pakistan. Pakistanis tend to read the U.S. rebalancing as a strategy aimed at containing China, one of Pakistan's only allies; tilting toward India, Pakistan's archenemy; and ignoring Pakistan.[24]

All told, the present U.S. approach of linking Pakistan with Afghanistan while excluding it from the wider Asian agenda feeds Pakistani anxieties in counterproductive ways. History suggests that insecurity has rarely led Islamabad to restraint, especially when it comes to the fear of Indian hegemony. As in the past, Pakistan's military is more likely to invest a disproportionate share of the state's resources in conventional arms and nuclear missiles, and more inclined to cling to militant and terrorist groups (like LeT) as asymmetrical tools to counter India's greater size and military might. To paraphrase Pakistan's former prime minister, Zulfikar Ali Bhutto, Islamabad would sooner "eat grass" than succumb to New Delhi's dominance. A future of grass eating would, of course, accelerate a vicious cycle of inadequate investment in Pakistan's people, domestic institutions, and infrastructure. It would render Islamabad even less capable of addressing the educational and economic aspirations of its people, and over time make it more vulnerable to revolutionary challengers at the local and national levels. Given Washington's concerns about the Pakistani nuclear program and terrorist networks—to say nothing of the U.S. interest in the wider region—these developments would be most unwelcome.

By instead adopting a strategy that emphasizes connections between Pakistan and U.S. interests in Asia's peace and economic growth, U.S. officials would more credibly signal Washington's long-term commitment to dealing with the various challenges that Pakistan presents, no matter what happens in neighboring Afghanistan. Simultaneously, by communicating a positive vision of Pakistan's integration into a peaceful and prosperous Asia, U.S. officials would be assisting Pakistan's development in ways that are likely to be more popular and effective than past U.S. assistance efforts.

To be sure, the success of this two-pronged strategy will depend on Pakistan's own policies and trajectory. If, despite U.S. efforts, Pakistan cannot or will not pursue a path toward peaceful regional economic integration, the United States would need to rely more heavily on the first prong of its strategy devoted to protecting U.S. interests in Asia from Pakistan-based security threats. Unwelcome as that scenario would be, at least a two-pronged strategy offers Washington a built-in fallback option.

Recommendations for U.S. Policy

To move away from the Af-Pak approach and implement a broader two-pronged Asia strategy for Pakistan, the United States should take the following military, diplomatic, and economic steps, all supported by a reorganization of the policymaking bureaucracy.

ADDRESS PAKISTAN-BASED THREATS TO REGIONAL SECURITY

To enable a long-term focus on Pakistan-based security threats to the wider Asian region, the United States should take the following steps:

- U.S. diplomats should quietly seek to initiate a dialogue on Pakistan with their Chinese counterparts in the Ministry of Foreign Affairs. Past crises in South Asia (political upheaval in Pakistan, Indo-Pakistani standoffs) have spurred episodic dialogues and cooperation between Washington and Beijing, so initial U.S. diplomatic overtures would recall those successes and stress the need to prevent similar scenarios. In addition, U.S. diplomats should continue to develop crisis management plans and protocols, including for the timely sharing of sensitive intelligence. Sessions should also be convened separately from other formal U.S.-China talks like the Strategic and Economic Dialogue in order to avoid the distractions of a perpetually overcrowded bilateral agenda.

- Starting with the national security adviser to the prime minister of India, senior U.S. national security officials should begin to discuss options for significantly expanded counterterror cooperation with their Indian counterparts, up to and including the possibility of basing U.S. military and/or intelligence operatives in India to address

Pakistan-based terrorist threats in a post-Afghanistan context. These conversations would be politically sensitive, so they should begin only after the next Indian government is elected in the spring. If diplomatic discussions make progress, the Pentagon should work with members of the U.S. intelligence community to develop specific implementation plans for on-the-ground operations in India.

- To prepare for a likely scenario in which neither Afghanistan nor India offers adequate basing opportunities for U.S. military and intelligence operations directed against Pakistan-based security threats, the Pentagon and CIA should identify and develop alternative sites, most likely on the Arabian Peninsula and at sea, where such efforts can be sustained and expanded as necessary over the long run. The cost of these bases, while considerable, would be less than retaining facilities in a violence-plagued Afghanistan and less likely to arouse Pakistani fears than bases in India.

- The Defense and State departments should work with Pakistan's new military and civilian leaders to plan post-2014 assistance to Pakistani forces involved in internal security operations and maintain training, equipment, and financial support at present levels. Congress should authorize and appropriate funds approaching the current amount of $400 million per year. Coalition Support Fund (CSF) "reimbursements" for Pakistani military operations in support of the international military presence in Afghanistan should be reduced, commensurate with the number of U.S. troops deployed there and the role Pakistan plays in promoting Afghan peace.

- Unlike the CSF, new U.S. military aid to Pakistan should not be linked primarily to the Afghanistan war. It should instead be conditioned on Pakistan's effort to address internal security threats, from the Pakistani Taliban to violent sectarian groups, and on Pakistan's overall commitment to countering violent extremism on its soil. Rather than an all-or-nothing approach of legislating formal conditionality on U.S. aid, Congress should, as it has in recent years, work closely with the White House and State Department to calibrate disbursements of military assistance in direct response to specific Pakistani policies and operations, encouraging and supporting constructive moves while simultaneously discouraging others.

SHIFT WASHINGTON'S PUBLIC MESSAGE TO PAKISTAN

The United States should clearly signal to Pakistan and other regional players how it intends to draw Pakistan into its broader Asian strategy though the following steps:

- The U.S. embassy in Islamabad should publicly highlight Washington's plans to include Pakistan in broader U.S. regional economic integration and development schemes as part of Washington's rebalancing strategy. Senior U.S. officials should include Pakistan in their list of rebalancing partners in Asia.

- The State Department should sponsor a Track II (nongovernmental) dialogue on the broader Asian region that includes Pakistani, Chinese, and Indian participants from relevant academic institutions and the private sector. The forum should begin by focusing on areas of mutual interest (such as scientific and technical education) while avoiding hot-button issues (such as Kashmir and other territorial disputes) to encourage participation. If the quadrilateral forum meets routinely and builds a network of regular participants, after several years it should invite official government participation and should also begin to tackle more divisive regional topics such as nuclear arms control, transit, energy, and water.

CREATE OPPORTUNITIES FOR PAKISTAN'S REGIONAL INTEGRATION

Although Washington cannot single-handedly enable Pakistan's integration in the wider Asian region, it should take the following steps to encourage such developments:

- U.S. diplomats and trade officials should negotiate a preferential U.S. trade access deal for India, Afghanistan, and Pakistan conditioned on reduced barriers to intraregional trade. Pakistan has long sought tariff-free access to the U.S. market for its textiles, but such deals have never made headway in Congress even though they are not expected to have any significant effect on U.S. consumers or producers. Looping India and Afghanistan into the effort would serve the dual purpose of improving prospects for enabling legislation and encouraging the Indo-Pakistani normalization process.[25]

- Nascent U.S. efforts to promote an "Indo-Pacific economic corridor" and a "new silk road" linking Afghanistan to Central Asia should be tied together through Pakistan.[26] To enable this, the State Department's bureaus of South and Central Asian Affairs and East Asia and Pacific Affairs; the Office of the Special Representative for Afghanistan and Pakistan, along with counterpart offices in the U.S. Agency for International Development (USAID); and, to a lesser extent, the Pentagon and Office of the U.S. Trade Representative should consult with their Pakistani counterparts in the working groups of the U.S.-Pakistan strategic dialogue to identify the infrastructural, regulatory, and political gaps that stand between these two regional initiatives. To secure outside funding and investment for connecting projects such as roads, border crossings, and power lines, U.S. and Pakistani diplomats should work together to approach the ADB and other potential funders, such as Japan. As the effort matures, U.S. diplomats should work with Pakistan to convene regional conferences (similar to the Regional Economic Cooperation Conferences on Afghanistan) to address remaining technical barriers to regional trade and transit.

- USAID and the State Department should lend financial and diplomatic support to the Turkmenistan-Afghanistan-Pakistan-India (TAPI) pipeline project. In addition to ongoing efforts to help the project achieve necessary private financing, U.S. diplomats in Kabul should convene the participating states to plan and fund security measures for pipeline construction in post-2014 Afghanistan, such as dedicated Afghan guard units, since the principal obstacle to progress is the threat of violence.

- Future U.S. civilian aid to Pakistan should be devoted to improving Pakistan's trade and transit infrastructure, especially its seaports and land ports, as well as promoting business development (through programs like USAID's Pakistan Private Investment Initiative).[27] To make this possible, the Obama administration should seek to retain funding levels near those authorized by existing legislation. However, given expectations of flat or declining U.S. assistance budgets, overall civilian assistance to Pakistan is unlikely to reach $1 billion per year. As a consequence, U.S. resources will need to be drawn from other

development projects in areas such as health and education. U.S. diplomats should approach European and Asian donors already active in
these sectors to make up for the shortfalls.

- Because Washington cannot single-handedly integrate Pakistan into
  Asia, development programs should be coordinated with Islamabad
  and U.S. funds should be conditioned on Pakistan's prior demon-
  stration of financial and political commitment to specific projects.
  U.S. officials should be clear that aid is politically sustainable only
  within a cooperative bilateral context but should avoid linking development aid to security issues over which Pakistan's civilian leaders
  lack control.

RESTRUCTURE U.S. POLICYMAKING BUREAUCRACY

To support the new strategy that removes Pakistan from the narrow
Af-Pak context and draws it into deliberations over wider regional
issues, the U.S. policymaking bureaucracy should be reconfigured in
the following ways, starting in early 2014:

- The State Department's special representative for Afghanistan and
  Pakistan (SRAP) should transition into a special envoy for Afghan
  reconciliation. Non-reconciliation SRAP responsibilities, including
  the management of Pakistan policy, should revert back to the Bureau
  of South and Central Asian Affairs (SCA), where they can be linked
  to a broader regional approach. In addition, deputy assistant secre-
  taries in SCA and the Bureau of East Asian and Pacific Affairs should
  be specifically tasked with coordinating policies that span East and
  South Asia.

- The National Security Staff (NSS) should be streamlined so that Pakistan will more likely be considered on its own terms (rather than first
  as a subset of the Af-Pak agenda) and as a part of a broader regional
  strategy that includes India. A special assistant to the president and
  coordinator for South Asia would oversee staff managing separate
  portfolios for India (along with Nepal, Sri Lanka, and Bangladesh),
  Pakistan, and Afghanistan.

- The Office of the Secretary of Defense for Policy should also be reconfigured to match the State Department and NSS. This would be accomplished by splitting the portfolio of the assistant secretary of defense for Asian and Pacific security affairs and naming a new assistant secretary of defense for South Asian security affairs. The new assistant secretary would have separate deputies for Pakistan, Afghanistan, and India.

Conclusion

A reoriented U.S. strategy for Pakistan is necessary, timely, and more likely than the current approach to advance U.S. aims in Pakistan and throughout the wider region.

Three factors necessitate the move away from a Pakistan strategy rooted in the post-9/11 Af-Pak agenda. First, U.S. involvement in Afghanistan is waning and Washington's claims of a long-term commitment to Afghanistan's future are not credible. Second, the U.S. interest in broader Asian developments, especially in encouraging continued economic growth, is undeniable. A strategy based upon such core U.S. interests will be both sustainable and credible. Third, Pakistan will continue to present significant potential threats to U.S. interests in wider Asia. A U.S. strategy for Asia that does not contemplate Pakistan's role is incomplete, and a U.S. strategy for Pakistan that primarily considers its role in the context of Afghanistan is shortsighted.

To argue that this strategic shift is timely is not to suggest that the business of Af-Pak is finished or that Washington can simply move on from the highly problematic issues of how to wind down its military presence and leave behind an Afghanistan with the greatest possible prospects for security and development. It is, however, to argue that to delay a strategic shift would only exacerbate Pakistan's confusion about its future relations with the United States in the post-2014 era, thus sowing counterproductive insecurities.

Moreover, this year's civilian and military leadership changes in Islamabad offer a natural opportunity to rethink and renegotiate the terms of the U.S.-Pakistan relationship. Pakistan's newly elected prime minister has clearly signaled his government's desire to focus on economic development, pursue peaceful relations with Pakistan's neighbors (including India), and rebuild a working relationship with the United States. All of these aims are constructive and consistent with a new, Asia-oriented Pakistan strategy.

The next session of the recently restarted U.S.-Pakistan strategic dialogue, scheduled to be held in early 2014, offers an ideal venue for senior U.S. policymakers to share plans and policies for Asia with their Pakistani counterparts and to explain how they perceive Pakistan's potential for a constructive role in those plans.[28] The dialogue should include a session in which State Department officials charged with managing East Asian and Pacific affairs brief the Pakistani side and respond to questions.

Admittedly, this new strategy presents U.S. policymakers with enormous implementation challenges. Yet the same would be true of any U.S. strategy that attempts to deal seriously with Pakistan. An Asia-oriented approach holds two significant advantages, however, when compared with the status quo. First, as hard as Washington may find it to incentivize and enable Pakistan's integration in Asia's wider economic success story, the challenge is far less daunting or costly than attempting to prop up Pakistan's economy through direct U.S. development assistance. Even the massive expansion of U.S. civilian assistance to Pakistan during the early Obama administration to $1.5 billion per year (authorized by the Kerry-Lugar-Berman legislation) pales in comparison to the potential resources that could be leveraged from expanding Pakistan's commercial ties with neighboring Asian states, starting with India. Washington can, at resource levels lower than those of the past several years, help to enable Pakistan's regional integration. However, success will come only if Pakistan's leaders also do their part. That cannot be taken for granted, but Islamabad does have good reasons to try, above and beyond any incentives Washington would offer. The remarkable development stories from other parts of Asia show that growth-driven transformation of entire societies is possible, even in the short span of a generation.

Second, and finally, by emphasizing trade more than aid and making a credible case for how the U.S.-Pakistan relationship will continue to matter over the long run, an Asia-centered strategy for Pakistan would be well received in Pakistan. That, in turn, would enhance prospects for bilateral cooperation across the board.

Endnotes

1. See Ashley J. Tellis and Aroop Mukharji, eds., "Is a Regional Strategy Viable in Afghanistan?" Carnegie Endowment for International Peace, 2011, http://carnegieendowment.org/files/regional_approach.pdf.
2. "Top Trading Partners, December 2012," U.S. Census Bureau, http://www.census.gov/foreign-trade/statistics/highlights/top/top1212yr.html.
3. "Major Foreign Holders of Treasury Securities," U.S. Department of the Treasury, http://www.treasury.gov/resource-center/data-chart-center/tic/Documents/mfh.txt.
4. Barack Obama, "Remarks to the Australian Parliament," Parliament House, Canberra, Australia, November 17, 2011, http://www.whitehouse.gov/the-press-office/2011/11/17/remarks-president-obama-australian-parliament; Hillary Clinton, "America's Pacific Century," *Foreign Policy*, November 11, 2011, http://www.foreignpolicy.com/articles/2011/10/11/americas_pacific_century.
5. For more on the White House's second-term vision for the rebalancing, see March 11, 2013, remarks by Thomas E. Donilon at http://asiasociety.org/new-york/complete-transcript-thomas-donilon-asia-society-new-york. On the economic aspects of the rebalancing, in particular the TPP, see remarks by Michael Froman, then deputy national security adviser for international and economic affairs, http://csis.org/files/attachments/120104_froman_tpp_keynote.pdf.
6. See, for instance, Vice President Joseph Biden's remarks on Asia-Pacific Policy, July 19, 2013, http://www.whitehouse.gov/the-press-office/2013/07/19/remarks-vice-president-joe-biden-asia-pacific-policy.
7. For the Bush administration's 2005 articulation of plans to support India's rise, see "Background Briefing by Administration Officials on U.S.-South Asia Relations," Office of the Spokesman, March 25, 2005, http://2001-2009.state.gov/r/pa/prs/ps/2005/43853.htm.
8. Stephen P. Cohen et al., *The Future of Pakistan* (Washington, DC: Brookings Institution Press, 2011).
9. The 1990s were marked by difficult discussions of this sort. See John W. Garver, *Protracted Contest: Sino-Indian Rivalry in the Twentieth Century* (Seattle: University of Washington Press, 2001), p. 330.
10. Lisa Curtis, "U.S. Should Press China to Abide by NSG Rules on Pakistani Nuclear Cooperation," Heritage Foundation, October 18, 2013, http://www.heritage.org/research/reports/2013/10/china-pakistan-and-the-nuclear-suppliers-group-commitments.
11. Indian prime minister Atal Bihari Vajpayee argued that Chinese nuclear assistance to Pakistan was a core cause of Indian insecurity in his letter to President Clinton after India's 1998 nuclear tests. See "Nuclear Anxiety; Indian's Letter to Clinton On the Nuclear Testing," *New York Times*, May 13, 1998, http://www.nytimes.com/1998/05/13/world/nuclear-anxiety-indian-s-letter-to-clinton-on-the-nuclear-testing.html.

12. Zvi Eckstein and Daniel Tsiddon, "Macroeconomic Consequences of Terror: Theory and the Case of Israel," *Journal of Monetary Economics* vol. 51, no. 5 (June 2004), pp. 971–1002.

13. For the direct costs of recent Indo-Pakistani military mobilizations, see Gaurav Kampani, "Placing the Indo-Pakistani Standoff in Perspective," Center for Nonproliferation Studies, Monterey Institute of International Studies, 2002, http://cns.miis.edu/reports/pdfs/indopak.pdf.

14. On the prospect that water scarcity will lead to Indo-Pakistani violence, see Brahma Chellaney, *Water: Asia's New Battleground* (Washington, DC: Georgetown University Press, 2011), p. 286.

15. For one constructive vision of such a strategy, see Maleeha Lodhi, "Wanted: A National Security Strategy," *The News*, May 7, 2013, http://www.thenews.com.pk/todays-news-9-175900-wanted-a-national-security-strategy. On hopes that Pakistan's new government may be up to the task, see Ahmed Rashid, " Sharif Faces Up to Saving Pakistan From Collapse," *Financial Times*, July 18, 2013, http://blogs.ft.com/the-a-list/2013/07/18/sharif-faces-up-to-saving-pakistan-from-collapse.

16. Ted Osius, "Enhancing India-ASEAN Connectivity," Center for Strategic and International Studies, June 2013, http://csis.org/files/publication/130621_Osius_EnhancingIndiaASEAN_WEB.pdf.

17. Rod Nordland, "U.S.-Pakistan Freeze Chokes Fallback Route in Afghanistan," *New York Times*, June 2, 2012, http://www.nytimes.com/2012/06/03/world/asia/us-pakistan-dispute-chokes-an-afghan-supply-route.html.

18. Greg Miller, Craig Whitlock, and Barton Gellman, "Top-Secret U.S. Intelligence Files Show New Levels of Distrust of Pakistan," *Washington Post*, September 2, 2013, http://www.washingtonpost.com/world/national-security/top-secret-us-intelligence-files-show-new-levels-of-distrust-of-pakistan/2013/09/02/e19d03c2-11bf-11e3-b630-36617ca6640f_story.html.

19. "Strengthening Our Partnership, Continuing Our Progress," USAID, August 2, 2013, http://www.usaid.gov/pakistan/usaid-in-pakistan-report.

20. "Counter-terror Cooperation With India High Priority: U.S.," *The Hindu*, July 9, 2011, http://www.thehindu.com/news/counterterror-cooperation-with-india-high-priority-us/article2213793.ece.

21. Sunil Khilnani et al., "Nonalignment 2.0: A Foreign and Strategic Policy for India in the Twenty-First Century," Centre for Policy Research, February 28, 2012, http://www.cprindia.org/workingpapers/3844-nonalignment-20-foreign-and-strategic-policy-india-twenty-first-century.

22. Michael Kugelman, "From Conundrum to Catastrophe?" National Bureau of Asian Research, March 13, 2013, http://www.nbr.org/research/activity.aspx?id=323.

23. See remarks by Deputy Secretary of Defense Ashton B. Carter, Center for Strategic and International Studies, Washington, DC, Monday, April 8, 2013, http://www.defense.gov/speeches/speech.aspx?speechid=1765.

24. This interpretation is based on interviews with officials at Pakistan's National Defense University and Ministry of Foreign Affairs, as well as with independent analysts in Islamabad, February 2013. For examples of this perspective, see also Munir Akram, "Shifting Asian Pivot," *Dawn*, April 28, 2013; Shehzad Qazi, "Hedging Bets: Washington's Pivot to India," *World Affairs Journal*, November/December 2012, http://www.worldaffairsjournal.org/article/hedging-bets-washington's-pivot-india.

25. Daniel S. Markey, "U.S. Should Remove Barriers to Trade With Pakistan, India," *Washington Post*, June 6, 2013, http://articles.washingtonpost.com/2013-06-06/opinions/39789374_1_nawaz-sharif-india-and-pakistan-daniel-markey.

26. On the Indo-Pacific Economic Corridor, see Robert Blake, "The Asia Rebalance: Why South Asia Matters," testimony before the House Foreign Affairs Committee, sub-committee on Asia and the Pacific, February 26, 2013, http://www.state.gov/p/sca/rls/rmks/2013/205210.htm.

27. "Pakistan Private Investment Initiative launched," *The Nation*, June 27, 2013, http://www.nation.com.pk/pakistan-news-newspaper-daily-english-online/business/27-jun-2013/pakistan-private-investment-initiative-launched.

28. Lesley Wroughton and Maria Golovnina, "U.S., Pakistan Agree to Start New Chapter in Long-Strained Relations," Reuters, August 1, 2013, http://www.reuters.com/article/2013/08/01/us-usa-pakistan-kerry-idUSBRE96U0Y920130801.

About the Author

Daniel S. Markey is senior fellow for India, Pakistan, and South Asia at the Council on Foreign Relations, where he specializes in security and governance issues in South Asia. He is the author of numerous publications, including a book on the future of the U.S.-Pakistan relationship, *No Exit from Pakistan: America's Tortured Relationship with Islamabad* (Cambridge University Press, 2013). From 2003 to 2007, Markey held the South Asia portfolio on the secretary's policy planning staff at the U.S. Department of State. Prior to government service, he taught in the department of politics at Princeton University, where he served as executive director of Princeton's research program in international security. Earlier, he was a postdoctoral fellow at Harvard's Olin Institute for Strategic Studies. Markey also served as project director of the CFR-sponsored Independent Task Force on U.S. strategy in Pakistan and Afghanistan. He earned a bachelor's degree in international studies from the Johns Hopkins University and a doctorate in politics from Princeton University.

Advisory Committee for
Reorienting U.S. Pakistan Strategy:
From Af-Pak to Asia

Walter Andersen
Paul H. Nitze School of Advanced
International Studies

Aysha A. Chowdhry
U.S. Senate Committee on Foreign Relations

Stephen P. Cohen
The Brookings Institution

Lisa Curtis
The Heritage Foundation

John A. Gastright
DynCorp International

Ziad Haider
Truman National Security Project

Seth G. Jones
RAND Corporation

Stephen R. Kappes
Torch Hill Investment Partners

Frank G. Klotz, *ex officio*
Council on Foreign Relations

Satu P. Limaye
East-West Center Washington

Mark E. Manyin
Congressional Research Service

Paul D. Miller
RAND Corporation

Robert J. Murray
CNA

Deepa Ollapally
Elliott School of International Affairs

Michael V. Phelan
U.S. Senate Committee on Foreign Relations

James Shinn
Princeton University

Andrew Small
German Marshall Fund of the United States

Paul B. Stares, *ex officio*
Council on Foreign Relations

Council Special Reports

Published by the Council on Foreign Relations

Afghanistan After the Drawdown
Seth G. Jones and Keith Crane; CSR No. 67, November 2013
A Center for Preventive Action Report

The Future of U.S. Special Operations Forces
Linda Robinson; CSR No. 66, April 2013

Reforming U.S. Drone Strike Policies
Micah Zenko; CSR No. 65, January 2013
A Center for Preventive Action Report

Countering Criminal Violence in Central America
Michael Shifter; CSR No. 64, April 2012
A Center for Preventive Action Report

Saudi Arabia in the New Middle East
F. Gregory Gause III; CSR No. 63, December 2011
A Center for Preventive Action Report

Partners in Preventive Action: The United States and International Institutions
Paul B. Stares and Micah Zenko; CSR No. 62, September 2011
A Center for Preventive Action Report

Justice Beyond The Hague: Supporting the Prosecution of International Crimes in National Courts
David A. Kaye; CSR No. 61, June 2011

The Drug War in Mexico: Confronting a Shared Threat
David A. Shirk; CSR No. 60, March 2011
A Center for Preventive Action Report

UN Security Council Enlargement and U.S. Interests
Kara C. McDonald and Stewart M. Patrick; CSR No. 59, December 2010
An International Institutions and Global Governance Program Report

Congress and National Security
Kay King; CSR No. 58, November 2010

Toward Deeper Reductions in U.S. and Russian Nuclear Weapons
Micah Zenko; CSR No. 57, November 2010
A Center for Preventive Action Report

Internet Governance in an Age of Cyber Insecurity
Robert K. Knake; CSR No. 56, September 2010
An International Institutions and Global Governance Program Report

From Rome to Kampala: The U.S. Approach to the 2010 International Criminal Court Review Conference
Vijay Padmanabhan; CSR No. 55, April 2010

Strengthening the Nuclear Nonproliferation Regime
Paul Lettow; CSR No. 54, April 2010
An International Institutions and Global Governance Program Report

The Russian Economic Crisis
Jeffrey Mankoff; CSR No. 53, April 2010

Somalia: A New Approach
Bronwyn E. Bruton; CSR No. 52, March 2010
A Center for Preventive Action Report

The Future of NATO
James M. Goldgeier; CSR No. 51, February 2010
An International Institutions and Global Governance Program Report

The United States in the New Asia
Evan A. Feigenbaum and Robert A. Manning; CSR No. 50, November 2009
An International Institutions and Global Governance Program Report

Intervention to Stop Genocide and Mass Atrocities: International Norms and U.S. Policy
Matthew C. Waxman; CSR No. 49, October 2009
An International Institutions and Global Governance Program Report

Enhancing U.S. Preventive Action
Paul B. Stares and Micah Zenko; CSR No. 48, October 2009
A Center for Preventive Action Report

The Canadian Oil Sands: Energy Security vs. Climate Change
Michael A. Levi; CSR No. 47, May 2009
A Maurice R. Greenberg Center for Geoeconomic Studies Report

The National Interest and the Law of the Sea
Scott G. Borgerson; CSR No. 46, May 2009

Lessons of the Financial Crisis
Benn Steil; CSR No. 45, March 2009
A Maurice R. Greenberg Center for Geoeconomic Studies Report

Global Imbalances and the Financial Crisis
Steven Dunaway; CSR No. 44, March 2009
A Maurice R. Greenberg Center for Geoeconomic Studies Report

Eurasian Energy Security
Jeffrey Mankoff; CSR No. 43, February 2009

Preparing for Sudden Change in North Korea
Paul B. Stares and Joel S. Wit; CSR No. 42, January 2009
A Center for Preventive Action Report

Averting Crisis in Ukraine
Steven Pifer; CSR No. 41, January 2009
A Center for Preventive Action Report

Congo: Securing Peace, Sustaining Progress
Anthony W. Gambino; CSR No. 40, October 2008
A Center for Preventive Action Report

Deterring State Sponsorship of Nuclear Terrorism
Michael A. Levi; CSR No. 39, September 2008

China, Space Weapons, and U.S. Security
Bruce W. MacDonald; CSR No. 38, September 2008

Sovereign Wealth and Sovereign Power: The Strategic Consequences of American Indebtedness
Brad W. Setser; CSR No. 37, September 2008
A Maurice R. Greenberg Center for Geoeconomic Studies Report

Securing Pakistan's Tribal Belt
Daniel S. Markey; CSR No. 36, July 2008 (Web-only release) and August 2008
A Center for Preventive Action Report

Avoiding Transfers to Torture
Ashley S. Deeks; CSR No. 35, June 2008

Global FDI Policy: Correcting a Protectionist Drift
David M. Marchick and Matthew J. Slaughter; CSR No. 34, June 2008
A Maurice R. Greenberg Center for Geoeconomic Studies Report

Dealing with Damascus: Seeking a Greater Return on U.S.-Syria Relations
Mona Yacoubian and Scott Lasensky; CSR No. 33, June 2008
A Center for Preventive Action Report

Climate Change and National Security: An Agenda for Action
Joshua W. Busby; CSR No. 32, November 2007
A Maurice R. Greenberg Center for Geoeconomic Studies Report

Planning for Post-Mugabe Zimbabwe
Michelle D. Gavin; CSR No. 31, October 2007
A Center for Preventive Action Report

The Case for Wage Insurance
Robert J. LaLonde; CSR No. 30, September 2007
A Maurice R. Greenberg Center for Geoeconomic Studies Report

Reform of the International Monetary Fund
Peter B. Kenen; CSR No. 29, May 2007
A Maurice R. Greenberg Center for Geoeconomic Studies Report

Neglected Defense: Mobilizing the Private Sector to Support Homeland Security
Stephen E. Flynn and Daniel B. Prieto; CSR No. 13, March 2006

Afghanistan's Uncertain Transition From Turmoil to Normalcy
Barnett R. Rubin; CSR No. 12, March 2006
A Center for Preventive Action Report

Preventing Catastrophic Nuclear Terrorism
Charles D. Ferguson; CSR No. 11, March 2006

Getting Serious About the Twin Deficits
Menzie D. Chinn; CSR No. 10, September 2005
A Maurice R. Greenberg Center for Geoeconomic Studies Report

Both Sides of the Aisle: A Call for Bipartisan Foreign Policy
Nancy E. Roman; CSR No. 9, September 2005

Forgotten Intervention? What the United States Needs to Do in the Western Balkans
Amelia Branczik and William L. Nash; CSR No. 8, June 2005
A Center for Preventive Action Report

A New Beginning: Strategies for a More Fruitful Dialogue with the Muslim World
Craig Charney and Nicole Yakatan; CSR No. 7, May 2005

Power-Sharing in Iraq
David L. Phillips; CSR No. 6, April 2005
A Center for Preventive Action Report

*Giving Meaning to "Never Again": Seeking an Effective Response to the Crisis
in Darfur and Beyond*
Cheryl O. Igiri and Princeton N. Lyman; CSR No. 5, September 2004

Freedom, Prosperity, and Security: The G8 Partnership with Africa: Sea Island 2004 and Beyond
J. Brian Atwood, Robert S. Browne, and Princeton N. Lyman; CSR No. 4, May 2004

Addressing the HIV/AIDS Pandemic: A U.S. Global AIDS Strategy for the Long Term
Daniel M. Fox and Princeton N. Lyman; CSR No. 3, May 2004
Cosponsored with the Milbank Memorial Fund

Challenges for a Post-Election Philippines
Catharin E. Dalpino; CSR No. 2, May 2004
A Center for Preventive Action Report

Stability, Security, and Sovereignty in the Republic of Georgia
David L. Phillips; CSR No. 1, January 2004
A Center for Preventive Action Report

Note: Council Special Reports are available for download from CFR's website, www.cfr.org.
For more information, email publications@cfr.org.